THE PRAYER OF JESUS

Juan López Vergara

Preface by Pope Francis

NOTES ON PRAYER

Volume 3

Our Sunday Visitor
Huntington, Indiana

Palazzo San Pio X, Via della Conciliazione, 5 00120 Città del Vaticano
www.pcpne.va; www.iubilaeum2025.va
Published 2024 by Our Sunday Visitor, Inc.

Our Sunday Visitor Publishing Division
Our Sunday Visitor, Inc.
200 Noll Plaza
Huntington, IN 46750
1-800-348-2440

ISBN: 978-1-63966-272-2 (Inventory No. T2938)
eISBN: 978-1-63966-273-9
LCCN: 2024948709

Cover and interior design: Amanda Falk
Cover art: Adobestock

OSV extends thanks to the Catholc Truth Society for its collaboration in producing this book.

Printed in the United States of America

Contents

Preface by Pope Francis

Prayer is the breath of faith, its most proper expression. It's like a silent cry that comes out from the heart of whoever trusts and believes in God. It's not easy to find words to express this mystery. How many definitions of prayer we can gather from the saints and masters of spirituality, as well as from the reflections of theologians! Nevertheless, it is always and only in the simplicity of those who live prayer that prayer finds expression. The Lord, moreover, warned us that, when we pray, we must not waste words, deluding ourselves that thus we will be heard. He taught us rather to prefer silence and to entrust ourselves to the Father, who knows the kind of things we need even before we ask for them (see Mt 6:7–8).

The Ordinary Jubilee of 2025 is already at the door. How to prepare ourselves for this event, so important for the life of the Church, if not by means of prayer? The year 2023 was set aside for a rediscovery of the conciliar teachings, contained especially in the four constitutions of the Second Vatican Council. It is a way of keeping alive the mandate that the Fathers gathered at the council wished to place in our hands, so that by means of its implementation, the Church might recover its youthful face and proclaim, in a language adapted to the men and women of our time, the beauty of the Faith.

Now is the time to prepare for a year that will be dedicated entirely to prayer. In our own time the need is being felt more and more strongly for a true spirituality capable of responding to the great questions which confront us every day of our lives, questions caused by a global scenario that is far from serene. The ecological-economic-social crisis aggravated by the recent pandemic; wars, especially the one in Ukraine, which sow death, destruction, and poverty; the culture of indifference and waste that tends to stifle aspirations for peace and solidarity and keeps God at the margins of personal and social life. ... These phenomena combine to bring about a ponderous atmosphere that holds many people back from living with joy and serenity. What we need, therefore, is that our prayer should rise up with greater insistence to the Father so that he will listen to the voice of those who turn to him, confident of being heard.

This year dedicated to prayer is in no way intended to affect the initiatives which every particular Church considers it must plan for in its own daily pastoral commitment. On the contrary, it aims to recall the foundation on which the various pastoral plans should be developed and find consistency. This is a time when, as individuals or communities, we can rediscover the joy of praying in a variety of forms and expressions. A time of consequence enabling us to increase the certainty of our faith and trust in the intercession of the Virgin Mary and the saints. In short, a year in which we can have the experience almost of a "school of prayer," without taking anything for granted (or at cut-rate), especially with regard to our way of praying, but making our own, every day, the words of the disciples when they asked Jesus: "Lord, teach us to pray" (Lk 11:1).

In this year we are invited to become more humble and to leave space for the prayer that flows from the Holy Spirit. It is he who knows how to put into our hearts and onto our lips the right words so that we will be heard by the Father. Prayer in the Holy Spirit is what unites us with Jesus and allows us to adhere to the will of the Father. The Spirit is the interior Teacher who indicates the way to follow. Thanks to him the prayer of even just one person can become the prayer of the entire Church, and vice versa. There is nothing like prayer according to the Spirit to make Christians feel united as the one family of God. It is God who knows how to recognize everyone's needs and how to make those needs become the invocation and intercession of all.

I am certain that bishops, priests, deacons, and catechists will find more effective ways this year of placing prayer as the basis of the announcement of hope which the 2025 Jubilee intends to make resonate in this troubled time. For this reason, the contribution of consecrated persons will be of great value, particularly communities of contemplative life. I hope that in all the shrines of the world, privileged places for prayer, initiatives should be increased so that every pilgrim can find an oasis of serenity and return with a heart filled with consolation. May prayer, both personal and communal, be unceasing, without interruption, according to the will of the Lord Jesus (see Lk 18:1), so that the kingdom of God may spread, and the Gospel reach every person seeking love and forgiveness.

As an aid for this Year of Prayer, some short texts have been produced which, with their simple language, will make possible entry into the various dimensions of prayer. I thank the authors for their contribution and willingly place into your hands these "notes" so that everyone can rediscover the beauty of trusting in the Lord with humility and joy. And don't forget to pray also for me.

Vatican City
September 27, 2023

Franciscus

Abba, your goodness has clouded my eyes, and from the depths of my heart I bless you

After thirty years spent in the silence and remoteness of an obscure village in Galilee, Jesus enters the desert and listens to the Baptist, a witness to the truth. John never refers to himself, but to someone greater than himself. The Nazarene comes to John as if he were the last of sinners, and bowing his head in humility he is baptized in the Jordan.

This unique experience of the fatherhood of God, whom he calls: *Abba* — which in his native Aramaic language means: Dad — will mark him forever, transforming his life!

Jesus is filled with the anointing of the goodness of the Spirit. It is a conversation that goes beyond ordinary experiences with his eternal Father, who dialogues with him, unveiling to him the marvelous mystery of his unique filiation:

In those days Jesus came from Nazareth of Galilee and was baptized by John in the Jordan. And when he came up out of the water, immediately he saw the heavens being torn open and the Spirit descending on him like a dove. And a voice came from heaven, "You are my beloved Son; with you I am well pleased." (Mark 1:9–11)

Abba, I meet you daily in prayer, where I breathe hope. I have asked myself not only about what you expect of me, about what I must do, for which you have sent me, but also about who I am. Today I experienced a culminating moment in my journey, when I came up out of the water, I saw the heavens being torn apart and the Spirit descending upon me. And I heard you tell me that I am your beloved Son.

What an amazing adventure to be your Son, *Abba,* in whom you are pleased!

The Spirit was the cause of the realization of this unique and sublime consciousness of filiation, which I heard from your lips, *Abba.*

Abba, I open my heart to you, who are the center of my life and the source of my existence, in order to understand what you have wished to tell me. I was filled with the Spirit, discovering myself as your beloved child, and the desire to do your will, to carry out your work, was kindled in me.

In an eternal instant, in that marvelous proximity to you, *Abba,* you have revealed to me the splendors of my divine filiation.

It is in this light that the mission of my life acquires its true dimension and is revealed in its spiritual and human depth: to be the witness of your paternity, and to share what you teach me. I feel consecrated and comforted by you, *Abba*, in this filial intimacy, which at the same time commences my mission.

Oh, *Abba,* your goodness has clouded my eyes, and from the depths of my heart, I bless you.

Abba, your Word is a torch for my footsteps

The soul of Jesus, the man who came from God, vibrated with the mystery dormant in his flesh. At a decisive moment, he made a choice that would consecrate him: to fulfill the will of God. Like every human choice, his also led to him enduring some trials, right after having experienced the favor of his *Abba*.

And Jesus, from his distinctive inner serenity, in a theological debate face to face with the *deceiver*, overcomes him, by resorting to the companion of his whole life: the divine Word, with the care of one who treats that which he loves. Jesus has conquered and will continue to conquer throughout his life.

Because he has undergone such a trial, he can help those who are experiencing it. He is in all things equal to men, except sin:

> Then Jesus was led up by the Spirit into the wilderness to be tempted by the devil. And after fasting forty days and forty nights, he was hungry. And the tempter came and said to him, "If

you are the Son of God, command these stones to become loaves of bread." But he answered, "It is written,

'Man shall not live by bread alone,
but by every word that comes
from the mouth of God.'

Then the devil took him to the holy city and set him on the pinnacle of the temple and said to him, "If you are the Son of God, throw yourself down, for it is written,

'He will command his angels concerning you,'

and

'On their hands they will bear you up,
lest you strike your foot against a stone.'"

Jesus said to him, "Again it is written, '*You shall not put the Lord your God to the test.*'" Again, the devil took him to a very high mountain and showed him all the kingdoms of the world and their glory. And he said to him, "All these I will give you, if you will fall down and worship me." Then Jesus said to him, "Be gone, Satan! For it is written,

'You shall worship the Lord your God
and him only shall you serve.'"

Then the devil left him, and behold, angels came and were ministering to him. (Matthew 4:1–11)

Abba, the moon shone brightly illuminating my footsteps, when the Spirit led me into the desert. At the end of forty days and forty nights of a beautiful stay, in intimate union with you, I remained with my eyes fixed on the exquisite sublimity of your face. And I was inhabited by the longing to prepare myself for my public ministry, discovering myself determined to fulfill your will.

I felt, *Abba*, deeply grateful. We spoke to each other from heart to heart.

When the sun began to give us its first rays, I felt hungry, *Abba*. I was so weak that I could hardly remain on my feet. However, at the same time I felt both weak and strong. A voice inside me told me that your Word is light, that it unveils our inner secrets, confronting us with the truth.

In a most brief instant, the adversary, an expert in slander, *Abba*, approached to test me. He spoke to me as if in a whisper, determined to make me fall, telling me that, if I was the Son of God, I should tell those stones to be turned into loaves of bread.

In the midst of such darkness, *Abba*, I abandoned myself to the mystery of your love. My parents used to insist that there is nothing nobler in life than a sublime memory. And my heart beat with one of them. It was my holy mother, who, at the dawn of a luminous day, transported by the power of the Spirit, with loving contemplative solicitude, savored the mystery of your Word. It always seemed that her soul was in prayer. Her eyes fused with mine, letting me know that your

Word had a name. She must have experienced this with great strength, to the point of knowing that she was the daughter of her Son.

Abba, I want nothing more than to be faithful to the mission you have entrusted to me, and to seek help in your Word, which has the power to give life to those who observe it faithfully.

In the gratuitousness of your love that affirms and sustains me and unites us forever, I rejected the *confuser*, assuring him that man does not live by bread alone, but by every word that comes from your mouth, *Abba.*

Faithful to my vocation, I put him in his place. He did not accept defeat, *Abba.* He submitted me again by leading me to Jerusalem. On the eaves of the Temple, he laid hold of your Word, confronting me with my identity, telling me, if I were the Son of God, to throw myself down, for it is written that you would entrust to your angels that my foot should not stumble on any stone.

I answered him by refusing to test you. Your Word, *Abba*, can deceive us if the spirit of obedience is lacking. And I made my own the words which you spoke one day through Moses, that you shall not tempt the Lord your God.

He took me to a mountain and showed me the inebriation that power can cause. He asked me to renounce worshiping you, *Abba.* To me, I exist in worshiping you! I commanded him to depart, saying to him, "You shall worship the Lord your God."

And he departed with the ill-taste of his failure, losing himself in the horizon, like a hideous stain. The prince of the world has no power over me. Your messengers came near and served me.

Abba, thank you because your Word was the torch for my footsteps, a light for my path.

Abba, today I confirmed that I am dreaming your own dreams

The time of Jesus was inaugurated with the power of the Spirit teaching in his synagogues. He is the teacher. He came to his beloved village of Nazareth, where he was conceived. There he grew up and became a man. In his modest house of prayer at the Sabbath liturgy, he began his work according to the will of the Spirit, with the certainty that Scripture contains the Word of God.

Jesus, born under the law, conformed to the ritual; and like any other Jew, he asked the head of the synagogue for permission to do the reading, bowed his head when he received the scroll of the prophet Isaiah, and found a passage in which he glimpsed what would be the blueprint of his life.

A magnificent text!

It is the great kerygmatic announcement that entails the fulfillment of prophecy. Jesus presented himself anointed by the Spirit of the Lord, as the herald of the Good News, sent to sow freedom, light, and grace.

His words were received with delight, but also with

a certain surprise, a symbol of the ministry of Jesus and the reactions he would provoke, foreshadowed in the oracle of Simeon.

Then, unexpectedly, they jumped from admiration to animosity, with hints of drama, and the son of Joseph rose to prominence, making his way over everyone:

> And he came to Nazareth, where he had been brought up. And as was his custom, he went to the synagogue on the Sabbath day, and he stood up to read. And the scroll of the prophet Isaiah was given to him. He unrolled the scroll and found the place where it was written,
>
> *"The Spirit of the Lord is upon me,*
> *because he has anointed me*
> *to proclaim good news to the poor.*
> *He has sent me to proclaim liberty to the captives*
> *and recovering of sight to the blind,*
> *to set at liberty those who are oppressed,*
> *to proclaim the year of the Lord's favor."*
>
> And he rolled up the scroll and gave it back to the attendant and sat down. And the eyes of all in the synagogue were fixed on him. And he began to say to them, "Today this Scripture has been fulfilled in your hearing." And all spoke well of him and marveled at the gracious words that were coming from his mouth. And they said, "Is not this Joseph's son?" And he said to

them, "Doubtless you will quote to me this proverb, 'Physician, heal yourself.' What we have heard you did at Capernaum, do here in your home town as well." And he said, "Truly, I say to you, no prophet is acceptable in his home town. But in truth, I tell you, there were many widows in Israel in the days of Elijah, when the heavens were shut up three years and six months, and a great famine came over all the land, and Elijah was sent to none of them but only to Zarephath, in the land of Sidon, to a woman who was a widow. And there were many lepers in Israel in the time of the prophet Elisha, and none of them was cleansed, but only Naaman the Syrian." When they heard these things, all in the synagogue were filled with wrath. And they rose up and drove him out of the town and brought him to the brow of the hill on which their town was built, so that they could throw him down the cliff. But passing through their midst, he went away. (Luke 4:16–30)

Abba, it has been a very intense day. Only in you rests my soul, from you comes my hope. From experience I know that behind every night comes a joyful dawn. To remain in prayer with you constitutes my innermost essence. You are a God who has a heart, you love with everlasting love, as the prophet has revealed to us.

The deepest and richest part of you, *Abba*, is your

goodness, a reflection of your mercy.

Abba, I love you with all my heart, with all my soul, with all my understanding, and with all my strength. I delight in your goodness. When I read the Holy Book, in a flash of divine truth, I understood that you had sent the prophet to announce to my exiled brothers and sisters that you would soon come to visit them. And I confirmed my vocation: to spread the hope of the Gospel to the poor, the captives, the blind, and the oppressed.

Anointed by the divine Spirit, I am beginning a new phase of my life, *Abba*. Without ceasing for a single moment to question myself, I have discovered that the action of the Spirit is the star that lightens my paths.

I am ready, *Abba*, to run after her!

The decisive course of my destiny impels me to boldly announce the Good News, *Abba*, a message that brings hope and dignity, particularly to so many who do not have what is necessary for a life that is fully human.

You desire mercy and not sacrifice, *Abba*.

These words have echoed in my soul since I was a young boy, when I sensed that a person's relationship with you was not based on how he spoke of you, *Abba*, but on how he treated his brothers and sisters.

Abba, every Saturday the attendant would allow my dad to approach the holy scrolls. He would kiss them with reverent piety. Stirring memories, I find myself laying my little head on his chest. In a spontaneous outburst he embraced me and kissed my forehead with the same reverent piety as he did the holy scrolls. In that eternal instant I felt my being glow with the intrinsic sacredness of the colors of mystery.

Yes, he was indeed a simple man, with the glory of the humble, convinced that life is beautiful and worth living. He was sensitive to the notes of your divine symphony: that is justice. And he did not assume justice, *Abba*, like many scribes. His justice, in a word, was love. The prevailing feeling toward him, which has inhabited my being since childhood, is permeated with enormous gratitude, dear *Abba*.

I stated with deep seriousness and gravity that today, *Abba*, this Scripture was fulfilled in the ears of those among whom I grew up, played, and worked. For more than thirty years my life was spent among them. They were astonished by my affirmation, but it was not enough for them; they wanted me to perform thc healings that I was said to have done in Capernaum. I was surprised by their unexpected reaction.

A bewildering turn of events, *Abba*!

They looked at me, *Abba*, with suspicion. For them I was still only the son of Joseph the carpenter. I broadened the horizon of my mission, reminding them of the saying that no prophet is welcomed by his people, until I finally evoked the prophets Elijah and Elisha, who also saved some pagans.

Abba, I felt a cold sweat running down my back. The reaction of those who knew me seemed unheard of, they wanted to throw me over the edge, but by the time I realized it, I had already left them behind. I bow my head before you, *Abba*, in deep prayer and withholding tears from flooding my heart at the thought of the immense sorrow that all this will cause my mother.

Abba, I did not find the Isaianic text by chance in the house of prayer, in the Sabbath liturgy, but under the guidance of the Spirit, with whom I am anointed. Now, I confess to you that it is the task for which I feel you have sent me, confirming to me that I dream your own dreams.

Abba, my mother hastened the beginnings of the Gospel

Mary, listener of the Word, a woman filled with gratitude, who had brought grace to John the Baptist, was changed after her meeting with Jesus in the Temple. Neither she nor her beloved husband understood this. The nature of her son's response made her return to Nazareth transformed, with a heartfelt deep understanding, for Mary kept all these things in her heart.

She knew that her son's life sprang from the living and eternal Word of God; and day by day he was nourished by it.

She could expect anything from him … !

This certainty built her up, carrying her life forward, making itself present in the first miracle manifesting the glory of her son and keeping her standing again on the scaffold of the cross.

Jesus' attitude was unique. His obedience in the vital domain of their home. How lovingly he cared for them! She would always keep a touching and grateful memory.

After his meeting with Philip and Nathanael, Jesus participates in the laughter and merriment of a wedding feast amidst singing and dancing. He sanctifies with his presence the conjugal union.

The wine is finished, and the flavor of a true feast is greatly missing! At the news, Mary's heart was startled, and, without saying more, she intervened, convinced that she was going to be cared for. Her son would provide the ultimate and best wine. And so, it was. He was the wine of the feast, symbol of a superior and transcendent event:

> On the third day there was a wedding at Cana in Galilee, and the mother of Jesus was there. Jesus also was invited to the wedding with his disciples. When the wine ran out, the mother of Jesus said to him, "They have no wine." And Jesus said to her, "Woman, what does this have to do with me? My hour has not yet come." His mother said to the servants, "Do whatever he tells you." Now there were six stone water jars there for the Jewish rites of purification, each holding twenty or thirty gallons. Jesus said to the servants, "Fill the jars with water." And they filled them up to the brim. And he said to them, "Now draw some out and take it to the master of the feast." So they took it. When the master of the feast tasted the water now become wine, and did not know where it came from (though the servants who had drawn

> the water knew), the master of the feast called the bridegroom and said to him, "Everyone serves the good wine first, and when people have drunk freely, then the poor wine. But you have kept the good wine until now." This, the first of his signs, Jesus did at Cana in Galilee, and manifested his glory. And his disciples believed in him.
>
> After this he went down to Capernaum, with his mother and his brothers and his disciples, and they stayed there for a few days. (John 2:1–12)

Abba, for the first time during my journey with you, today I hesitated before the words of my mother, who with audacious joy told me that the wine for the feast was finished. Despite that love of a little boy who adores his mother, which has never ceased to throb in my heart, I rejected her.

Her words, *Abba,* did not fit my life plan!

She, with that serenity so much hers, *Abba,* impregnated with tenderness, which springs from her clean and humble heart, took no notice, and ordered the servants to do as I told them.

And although my process was undergoing an agitation, *Abba,* I felt a perceptible ray of light circulating between my mother's words. Her words awakened my amazement with the fire of her love. I knew that her request was inspired and inspiring.

Abba, my soul expanded. I received the lesson from

my most holy mother. She has remained forever filled with your grace and amazed by your Word.

The more I am in your intimacy, in prayer with you, *Abba*, the more I savor the marvelous scope of my mission. A mission mysteriously invested with glory, a glory that I manifested to those who were beginning to discover me.

And I manifested my glory, *Abba*, by doing good, by restoring joy to that couple.

My greatest hope, *Abba*, is that through these signs they will believe that I have been sent by you; that they will inspire faith in my mission. In them beats the immense mystery of the most authentic love. Through them I reveal your face, revealing myself as your supreme witness of the glory I have received from you.

Abba, my most holy mother, intervened with that smile of hers, and, giving life to her prophetic words, she hastened the beginning of the Gospel.

Abba, your providential love embraces everything

Among the houses, the squares, the crowded streets, Jesus was thinking how his existence had become interwoven with the threads of attachments and detachments. He withdrew in search of solitude. A deep and constant desire inhabited him, it was essential for him to be with his *Abba*. His prayer was incessant and tireless!

His parents taught him to grow with serenity and trust, to seek God in his own existence, to abandon himself in his hands. When he went to sleep, he was calm as a weaned child in his mother's arms.

Since he was a young boy, he sought solitude in remote places, spending hours in silence, in the presence of God, whom he invoked as *Abba*. His existence had passed with such simplicity, that his countrymen would be astonished by his wisdom and the miracles performed by his hands. Jesus was willing to give up, even his own life, as redemption on behalf of many.

The free detachment, which is the wellspring of

fruitfulness, rushed one day at the sight of a little bird, soaring upward, embracing the heavens. How he loved to reflect on the goodness of God, who was at work in the innermost part of life:

> No one can serve two masters, for either he will hate the one and love the other, or he will be devoted to the one and despise the other. You cannot serve God and money.
>
> Therefore I tell you, do not be anxious about your life, what you will eat or what you will drink, nor about your body, what you will put on. Is not life more than food, and the body more than clothing? Look at the birds of the air: they neither sow nor reap nor gather into barns, and yet your heavenly Father feeds them. Are you not of more value than they? And which of you by being anxious can add a single hour to his span of life? And why are you anxious about clothing? Consider the lilies of the field, how they grow: they neither toil nor spin, yet I tell you, even Solomon in all his glory was not arrayed like one of these. But if God so clothes the grass of the field, which today is alive and tomorrow is thrown into the oven, will he not much more clothe you, O you of little faith? Therefore do not be anxious, saying, 'What shall we eat?' or 'What shall we drink?' or 'What shall we wear?' For the Gentiles seek after all these things, and

> your heavenly Father knows that you need them all. But seek first the kingdom of God and his righteousness, and all these things will be added to you.
>
> Therefore do not be anxious about tomorrow, for tomorrow will be anxious for itself. Sufficient for the day is its own trouble. (Matthew 6:24–34)

Abba, in your presence, in prayer with you, in light of your truth that beams upon me, as I enter into your project, into the foundations of your messianic reign, I have the feeling that true life is elsewhere, for I have learned that wealth is almost always unjust.

How can I answer your call, *Abba,* which exhorts me to defend the lowliest!

From this has sprung my severe criticism of those who hoard wealth without a thought for those in need. A power that wins the heart by chaining it, by turning it away from you, *Abba,* who, I insist, are the light of our life, who knows what we need, before we ask you for it.

You constantly watch over us, *Abba,* attending to what we need in order to live.

On this path of searching, I am excited by the celestial mantle of your goodness that protects everything, *Abba.* It is an absolute principle, like a miraculous wind, that fills my soul with joy. You are the creator of all that is visible and also of that which we do not see, and you do not cease to lavish with loving care the work emanating from your Word.

Abba, today I went up the mountain and, as the teacher that I am, I sat down. And I shared with a multitude of people, surrounded by my disciples, what I contemplated with you: the enchantment of your creative action. The love that sustains your creation is never finished, inciting us to turn our gaze toward eternity, which is the dimension that corresponds to the infinite measure of love.

Your love is creator, dear *Abba*.

I believe, *Abba*, in your love. And with greater depth grows in me the consciousness of absolute dependence on you, which frees me toward wider horizons.

I exhorted them to learn to look beyond themselves, *Abba*, to grow with confidence in the goodness of life, to not worry about the future anymore than the birds.

And among the many surprises I had today, *Abba*, I was ecstatic to observe one of these small lilies. This striking flower with its elongated leaves spoke to me in words of almost heartbreaking beauty. Yes, your creation, *Abba*, is like an open book that speaks to me of you. And the grace of its expression never detracts from the depth of its message: the little birds and the plants, in proof of gratitude, live giving praise to you, their Creator.

In an attitude oriented toward the infinite, I turn my eyes toward you, *Abba*, persuaded that trust is the intimate incentive in the search for your project, for your reign. This must be the primary element in the life of the disciples you have entrusted to me.

Abba, to the certainty of knowing that I am your beloved Son, your Chosen One, I must add the certainty that your providential love embraces everything.

Abba, I ask you to give courage and enthusiasm to those who decide to follow me

Jesus, tireless teacher, moves in the midst of the people and, suddenly, urges them to make a decision in his favor. Although his authority is surprising, his disciples do not know what to think, feeling his word is sharper than a two-edged sword. Following him demands a decision in favor of Jesus. This is the sword of decision before which a man is confronted, even with the members of his family. Was Jesus not considered mad by his own relatives? This announcement would have significant repercussions in some followers who, stunned, would decide to abandon him:

> Do not think that I have come to bring peace to the earth. I have not come to bring peace, but a sword. For I have come to set a man against his father, and a daughter against her mother, and a daughter-in-law against her mother-in-law. And a person's enemies will be those of his

> own household. Whoever loves father or mother more than me is not worthy of me, and whoever loves son or daughter more than me is not worthy of me. (Matthew 10:34–37)

Abba, in the intimacy I have experienced with you, as I direct my soul toward you, with the desire to do your will, I perceive that I carry within me an overflowing mystery. This mystery implies transcending the present in its totality, which is why I consider prayer to be indispensable. This mystery carries with it a filial meaning, which impels me to question in depth the freedom of my disciples.

I do not want to forget, *Abba,* the fundamental experience of my life: to be your Son. As for such a relationship, I experience it in a vivid way: the heavens were torn apart; since then, a new dawn began to shine, illuminated by your voice.

Yes, that was your true voice! And I discovered myself as your beloved Son, *Abba.*

Today, *Abba,* I announced one of the most painful experiences that those who are willing to follow me may have to face. Their decision may affect their family, destroying relationships, causing animosity among their own relatives, and I exhorted them to love me more than their parents and children. Does it not belong to my vocation to unfold your potential, *Abba,* by giving all that you can give through me to those whom you have asked to listen to me? In me acts that eternal love, so much yours, which assures life, promising infinity.

As I look back over the stages of my journey, I am aware that, from my experience of filiation, *Abba*, through a precious grace of fruitfulness, I perceive myself as similar to you.

It is in the heart of this experience, *Abba*, that my identity beats, an identity that I sense more and more clearly, my being a son.

At midnight and in the most splendid silence, I ask you, my dear *Abba*, to give courage and enthusiasm to those who decide to follow me.

Abba, I taught them that learning to pray is learning to hope, and therefore learning to live

Jesus' actions in his Galilean homeland were characterized by his continuous travels through cities and villages, announcing the reign of God. He was accompanied by his inner circle of disciples and a significant group of women. The impression caused by his encounters with God, whom he invoked as his *Abba*, was enormous.

Jesus of Nazareth preached about the God of Abraham, Isaac, and Jacob, a God of the living. With much intensity he emphasized his kind and merciful fatherhood, opening wonderful perspectives!

From the heart of the man who came from God flowed a wellspring of mercy for each one of his brothers and sisters, giving life to the name that God gave him through the lips of the angel.

He used to remain in prayer from midnight until dawn, convinced that he who knows how to pray well knows how to live well. His message was inseparable from his person. He revealed God's being with his own ways of acting.

He was the man for others!

One of his disciples asked him to teach them to pray as John taught his own disciples, the one whom Jesus had referred to as the greatest man among those born of women. Jesus answered with brevity, precision, and complete transparency:

> Now Jesus was praying in a certain place, and when he finished, one of his disciples said to him, "Lord, teach us to pray, as John taught his disciples." And he said to them, "When you pray, say:
>
> 'Father, hallowed be your name. Your kingdom come. Give us each day our daily bread, and forgive us our sins, for we ourselves forgive everyone who is indebted to us. And lead us not into temptation.'" (Luke 11:1–4)

Abba, I have spent a great part of the night in prayer, in contemplative solitude with you, in whom I have placed my hope. My love for you, *Abba,* grows continually. Thank you with all my heart for welcoming me.

I need so much to be with you, *Abba*!

Your touch accompanies me, *Abba*, and determines me. It arouses a great peace in my soul. I want to live only for you, with you and in you.

I was cherishing the idea of speaking to them about the importance of prayer, *Abba*, and one of my disciples asked me to teach them how to pray.

The first thing was to teach them to call you *Abba*, to express their status as sons and daughters and, of course, their being brothers and sisters.

In my home in Nazareth, *Abba*, I learned that no people is as close to you as ours. It is your holy people, consecrated to you, whom you chose, from whom comes salvation. This memory, *Abba*, left an indelible impression, which has shaped me forever.

My dad had a pleasant but solemn character. He radiated peace, *Abba*. The fear of you was the beginning of his wisdom, he experienced your holiness.

Abba, his soul was turned toward you!

Oh, what confidence he had in your loving fidelity, *Abba*. In the midst of his intense, vigilant, and patient work, he stood out for his simplicity and desire to serve. He loved life, living with magnificent freedom of spirit.

How can I forget his eyes, *Abba*, and his hands that broke bread, and welcomed or corrected me. I have maintained a deep affection for him. There is an even greater reason for joy: he kept a mystery, *Abba*, which I could perceive settling in his soul at the end of the day, when, believing that I was asleep, he would go to my bed to give me a last kiss, and would say a prayer.

In one of those cold winters, he died of a sudden illness, but his faith lives on in me. His departure rekindled my family feelings. It taught me that without trust one cannot live. Trust is communion. And that immense faith, open to your immensity, is one of the sweetest blessings I have received from you, *Abba*, through Dad, whom I remember with ever-renewed admiration.

With my eyes turned inward, I feel an irresistible impulse to call you *Abba*. To invoke you in this way invades the most intimate part of my being, awakening a new sense, which originates in me an immense freedom, an immense joy, an immense peace.

I have no other ambition, *Abba*, but to consecrate my life to you, to consummate the mission you have entrusted to me, which demands a radical commitment. My truth is a desire for you and an openness to carry out your will, which consists in making your name known to them.

That is why, in the enchantment of that moment, *Abba*, I emphasized the importance of sanctifying your name and asking for the coming of your kingdom.

Yes, *Abba*, your name and your kingdom!

To lift up our eyes to you, to perceive the dimensions of reality. Isn't prayer the school of hope, its initiation, its language, and its interpretation? *Abba*, I taught them that whoever prays hopes in your goodness and in your power, which are beyond their means.

Abba, prayer is hope in action, so that earth may become heaven.

I immediately announced three petitions that shed light on the evidence of your fatherhood, *Abba*, as the father who gives bread, who desires that we live in peace with our neighbor, who forgives sins, who defends his children from deception.

In the mirror of hope we see the essence of your love, and your love, *Abba*, is a love without reservation. Your love is creative and includes an inexhaustible readiness to forgive. No more an eye for an eye and a tooth for a tooth, but to transform evil with the power of forgiveness.

Abba, I taught them that by turning their longings into invocations, from their being pilgrims, detached from everything, they will experience you in a new way, turning their daily anxieties into hope.

I asked them, *Abba*, when they prayed, to ask you for forgiveness for their sins, and to be ready to forgive everyone who owed them. And I also advised them to pray to you, *Abba*, that you would not abandon them in temptation.

You are humble and gentle, *Abba*, at the same time omnipotent and just!

Temptation is a trial, although it is understandable as an education in fidelity, in pure love, in authentic faith. I myself, *Abba*, from my own experience, know how important it is to be with you, enlightened by your Word, at the moment of temptation.

Abba, with the satisfaction of a work accomplished, I taught them that learning to pray is learning to hope, and therefore learning to live.

Abba, I bless you, you have entrusted and transmitted everything to me

In a context of unbelief, Jesus has been rejected. His identity is the underlying issue. Even the messengers of John the Baptist asked him if he was the One who was to come or if they should wait for someone else. Jesus sees around him people who have welcomed him and listen to his word. He calls them "little ones"!

These are the people around him who are tired and oppressed. They have been forced to carry unbearable loads, an accumulation of precepts that enslave them. These constraints have been imposed by the wise and arrogant that know the Law of Moses, yet they have rejected Jesus.

He finds a source of hope in the little ones, who have known how to receive the revelation of the Father, manifested in his actions and words. And, as he looks at them, he perceives the presence of his Father, and a blessing of praise and gratitude flows forth from his desire to show his ways to the humble. Jesus reveals himself to be the only one who knows the Father and the only one who can reveal him through his testimony.

He presents himself as a model and teacher, the bearer of the wisdom of the Father, who gives himself to the little ones, thus awakening their deepest sleep, motivating their call:

> At that time Jesus declared, "I thank you, Father, Lord of heaven and earth, that you have hidden these things from the wise and understanding and revealed them to little children; yes, Father, for such was your gracious will. All things have been handed over to me by my Father, and no one knows the Son except the Father, and no one knows the Father except the Son and anyone to whom the Son chooses to reveal him." (Matthew 11:25–27)

Abba, in the enchantment of the mountain illuminated by the shining of the stars, in prayer I perceive your mystery, which, in bringing to light the face of your desires, instills in me a feeling of complete gratitude. And I perceive everywhere the liveliness of your presence. It increases the intensity of the love written for you in my soul, which nourishes the union of my being with you.

Abba, how much I understand when I become aware of such a bond! I bless you as I live deeply my faith. With my heart clothed in joy, I will give thanks to you, praising you forever.

You reject the arrogance of not a few scribes and priests, *Abba*, the power of the Gospel is hidden from them, and, instead, you reveal it to us little ones. As we turn our souls to you, we experience that everything that comes from you is sweet, humble, serene.

Abba, leaning over your soul, from my lowliness, I bless the fullness of conscience that makes me see that everything has been given to me by you. In this experience, *Abba*, I perceive that no one loves me as you do and no one loves you as I do, that I receive from you the mission to reveal and fulfill the name that you have assigned to me.

The little ones who open their hearts with an insatiable yearning for life, ready to listen to me, delight you, *Abba*.

I have announced to them, *Abba*, that your desire is to see them happy, free from hunger and oppression!

Abba, the sick believed again that you are the God of life. They have discovered what is essential and, through your spiritual anointing, they trust in me. The joy that is bound up in this gesture of surrender, *Abba*, makes them know that they have everything if they have me, because you have entrusted everything to me, and I do nothing on my own but what I see you do.

Abba, I, Jesus of Nazareth, your beloved Son, your Chosen One, bless you with all my heart. You have entrusted and transmitted everything to me.

Abba, today I encouraged them to come to me

Jesus embraced in his soul the mystery of his divine filiation. This mystery did not suppress the constraints of his humanity. Like us, he always needed to love and to be loved. He did not cease to grow for a single day of his life in wisdom and grace before God and mankind.

In baptism he was graced to know that he was the beloved Son, in whom his Father was well pleased, and that he received in his humanity the fullness of the Spirit.

Thus he inaugurated the messianic times with a proposition that turns the world upside down, making his follower's hearts vibrate by exhorting them:

> Come to me, all who labor and are heavy laden, and I will give you rest. Take my yoke upon you, and learn from me, for I am gentle and lowly in heart, and you will find rest for your souls. For my yoke is easy, and my burden is light. (Mat-

thew 11:28–30)

Abba, mindful of your love, the source of life, which configures my heart to yours, I am able to feel a clamor of unity vibrating in me as an expression of gratitude. Within me your love vibrates with all its strength, establishing the most precious relationship, a mystery of communion that overflows me, enlightening my identity.

As I read the book of my life in prayer, I look back over all the years full of gratitude and hope, for you have written each page together with me. *Abba,* I see that you have always been with me.

Today, *Abba,* my soul was moved by the thought of my brothers and sisters being denied the opportunity to meet with you.

Abba, you gave me words of encouragement to speak to the afflicted. When I offered them to come to me in order to give them rest, I felt joy flowing in my whole being. An extreme joy, which clarifies my mission, do the strong need a physician? In complete harmony and peace with you, I look at each person, seeking their good.

Being meek and small, of humble extraction, *Abba,* as my mother has always considered herself, I presented myself to them as the Teacher.

And, *Abba,* I invited them to come to me and fearlessly become my disciples, bearing my yoke. Thus I offered rest for their souls. Not because I demanded less, but because I demanded the essential: the love that liberates, following in the footsteps of my filial obedience, for I have shared nothing other than what I have heard from you.

Having received from you such a mission, which I much exercise from love, solidarity, and service, *Abba*, today I encouraged them to come to me.

Abba, Peter's words stirred my soul

To the north, by the springs of the Jordan, lies Caesarea Philippi, where Jesus questioned his followers about his identity. His testimony radiated a creative force. The question had long been circulating among them:

"Who is this man?"

First, he asked them what others were saying about him. Then he questioned them directly. Simon, in the name of the whole group, proclaimed the messiahship of his Master. Jesus congratulated him. And he announced to him that the Father had chosen him to carry out his work in the world, that he had upon him the task of founding his Church:

> Now when Jesus came into the district of Caesarea Philippi, he asked his disciples, "Who do people say that the Son of Man is?" And they said, "Some say John the Baptist, others say Elijah, and others Jeremiah or one of the prophets." He said to them, "But who do you say that I am?" Simon Peter replied, "You are the Christ, the Son

> of the living God." And Jesus answered him, "Blessed are you, Simon Bar-Jonah! For flesh and blood has not revealed this to you, but my Father who is in heaven. And I tell you, you are Peter, and on this rock I will build my church, and the gates of hell shall not prevail against it. I will give you the keys of the kingdom of heaven, and whatever you bind on earth shall be bound in heaven, and whatever you loose on earth shall be loosed in heaven." Then he strictly charged the disciples to tell no one that he was the Christ. (Matthew 16:13–20)

Abba, during my arduous journey I have been sustained by a deep trust in you. In prayer you always listen to me. I have found that, unlike the fragile answers, the questions are appropriate, especially those that inquire into the meaning of our being.

I rejoice in your presence, *Abba*, happy to be with you, who know me from the innermost part of myself, just as your beloved Son knows you from the innermost part of yourself. I have opened my eyes to the Spirit, who kindles within me the fire of your love.

Today, *Abba*, I questioned my disciples about who people say that the Son of Man is. They told me that some, like the wicked Herod Antipas, believed him to be the resurrected John the Baptist. Others that he was Elijah, and still others Jeremiah, the suffering prophet, or one of the prophets.

Abba, people's opinions do not agree with my identity. Although there is some truth in some of their perceptions, for to conceptualize me as a prophet is equivalent to recognizing a divine mission.

I immediately asked them their personal opinion, *Abba*. And Simon uttered these words: "You are the Christ, the Son of the living God."

Abba, I heard the spokesman of my apostles say this truth that nestles within me. And I changed his name, just as you changed Abram's. A change of name is equivalent to a change of destiny. And I made him an exceptional promise, by placing in his hands the keys of your kingdom.

You had told me, *Abba*, with that eloquence of yours, discreet to the letter, what I heard today from the lips of the spokesman of my apostles.

Abba, the overwhelming force of his dazzling words stirred the very depths of my soul.

Abba, I proclaimed that unless a grain of wheat dies, it remains just a grain of wheat

The situation was getting worse by the day. Jesus loved his people and was committed to the defense of the least of them. He announced their right and their duty to be happy. This had a price! In a short time, Jesus had to learn to be as simple as a dove and as wise as a serpent. He knew he was in the midst of wolves. With his mind fixed on his Father, obedient to the task he received from him, he integrated his violent death into his mission of service, offering his life as a ransom for all. A brave man!

And an evolution in his desire to fulfill what the Father asked of him, led him to proclaim his resurrection, not without first having to go through the Way of the Cross. When his Master announced a plan that surpassed his own projects, the first among his followers took him aside and began to rebuke him.

Peter even dared to scold him whom he had confessed as "the Christ," the Holy One of God who has the words of eternal life. The Son of Man put Peter in his place:

> And he began to teach them that the Son of Man must suffer many things and be rejected by the elders and the chief priests and the scribes and be killed, and after three days rise again. And he said this plainly. And Peter took him aside and began to rebuke him. But turning and seeing his disciples, he rebuked Peter and said, "Get behind me, Satan! For you are not setting your mind on the things of God, but on the things of man." (Mark 8:31–33)

Abba, how many times in prayer, not without reverential trust, between moaning and weeping, I have begged you to let the chalice pass from me, but not to do my will, but yours. My feelings have been mixed. To the extent that I almost broke inside, conscious that they were going to kill me, I, who have dedicated my existence to reflect your goodness.

Abba, through a unifying gaze you aroused in my being the hope that my tears would have an answer. In these I have found an outlet. They are a precious gift of yours. And you, *Abba,* you listened to me!

In the life of the Spirit, I identify myself with the prayer of my older brothers, meditating that every tear will have its reward. But I have found myself again, *Abba*, feeling the fresh breath of your love, with a verse of the psalm with which my people celebrate the victory achieved by you, the one that speaks of the stone that the builders rejected and ended up becoming the cornerstone.

Abba, sensing the hidden meaning of suffering, I considered that it was the moment to teach them that it was necessary for me to suffer and be accused by the leaders and the chief priests and the teachers of the law, and that I would be resurrected three days later.

Abba, death is but the gateway to the fullness of life.

The spokesman for my apostles, *Abba*, did not understand that in order to be resurrected it would be necessary to go through the path of suffering. I was forced to reprimand him. I ordered him to return to his rightful place: to be a disciple.

Today, finally, *Abba*, I proclaimed that unless a grain of wheat dies, it remains just a grain of wheat.

Abba, today I revealed that whoever decides to come after me, after suffering, will see the light

On his way, Jesus stopped, suffering and terrified, imagining himself on the cross, dying the death of a subversive slave. He lived to the depths of humanity. For how long and how many times, with reverent attitude, he had to live in a state of clamor and tears, divine and human tears of the man who came from God, which intertwine destinies of death and resurrection.

The cross will become the sign of the Christian, and his greatest title of glory.

After making the first announcement of the Passion and Resurrection, Jesus, absolutely innocent, in the presence of those who listened to him, manifested the conditions for following him. Upon hearing the mystery that embraces self-offering, some were stunned. Jesus warned that whoever was ashamed of him and of his words would not be recognized when he came in his glory, in his Father's glory:

> And he said to all, "If anyone would come after me, let him deny himself and take up his cross daily and follow me. For whoever would save his life will lose it, but whoever loses his life for my sake will save it. For what does it profit a man if he gains the whole world and loses or forfeits himself? For whoever is ashamed of me and of my words, of him will the Son of Man be ashamed when he comes in his glory and the glory of the Father and of the holy angels. But I tell you truly, there are some standing here who will not taste death until they see the kingdom of God." (Luke 9:23–27)

Abba, at the light of dawn, I want to meditate with you. I need you so much! I want to thank you for the gift of prayer. Thank you for receiving me, for welcoming me, for listening to me, for understanding me. In these moments of encounter, a lively inner knowledge of you illuminates the mystery and fills my soul with gratitude. There are so many memories that time also revalues.

Gratitude, *Abba*, is the memory of the heart!

You are the God of tenderness and solidarity, my dearest *Abba*. Your goodness enfolds my mystery, inviting me to reflect it in every act of my life. I trust in your love, my heart rejoices in doing your will.

Your love, *Abba*, is everything for me!

I felt compelled to clarify that whoever longs to live

the utopia of the Gospel, *Abba*, would have to follow me, come out of himself, and take up his cross. It is a tremendous comparison, for it alludes to the condemned who drag the wood on which they are to be nailed.

Abba, I encouraged them to renew their decision every day, through humble discernment, in active vigilance, which calls for fidelity.

But having fixed my eyes on the mystery of suffering, I spoke of the cross that you, *Abba*, offer to each one of us. That which does not involve dragging it by force, but loving it, because you have willed it so. And my disciples must do it in my company, following me.

If it were not for the prayer with which I try to keep myself united to you, *Abba*, it would have been impossible for me to announce your greatest desire: that those who lose their lives for me, your beloved Son, in whom you are pleased, will find it.

I helped them see that behind the quest to save their lives, there are latent dangers of returning to the surface of prosperity, power and money. Another path involves the violence of love. And the most beautiful way to live is to make others happy without expecting anything in return, following the example of you, *Abba*, who are good even to the ungrateful and the perverse.

But such a thing is not improvised, *Abba*, it implies entering into themselves, conscious of being in your presence, to see that it is by surrendering their life that they can continue to live.

Abba, only surrendering eternizes!

Thank you, *Abba*, for this impulse of generosity that you awaken in me, for I have come not to be served but to serve and to give my life for the redemption of many.

In renouncing, *Abba*, in their willingness to sacrifice, in taking up their cross, they will acquire a good of much greater value, the happiness of detachment.

Abba, from my experience of you and also from my experience with my brothers and sisters, especially the poorest, with whom I share their sufferings, I announced that whoever would be ashamed of me by abandoning the way of the Gospel, when I return in your glory, I will not recognize.

It is necessary that those who decide to follow me, *Abba*, give testimony of their faith, giving life to the demands of the Good News. I announced that their future depended on their fidelity!

Before you, *Abba*, before the mystery of all that I am and live and feel, my heart throbbed, when I announced that some of those who accompanied me would not taste death until they saw the kingdom of God.

Today I revealed, *Abba*, that whoever decides to come after me, after suffering, will see the light.

Abba, I bless you for confirming my primary mission

Jesus questioned his disciples about who the people said he was, and even more so who they themselves said he was. Peter affirmed that he was the Christ of God. And Jesus, referring to himself as the Son of Man, announced for the first time that he would have to suffer, be put to death, and on the third day rise again.

He urged them to choose him, and carrying their own cross, to follow him.

A few days later, taking with him Peter, John, and James, he went up the mountain to pray. And as Jesus prayed, the Father manifested him as his Son, to whom they were to listen. His glory shone like lightning and was reflected in his Chosen One. He was transfigured by divine love:

> Now about eight days after these sayings [Jesus] took with him Peter and John and James and went up on the mountain to pray. And as he was praying, the appearance of his face was altered,

> and his clothing became dazzling white. And behold, two men were talking with him, Moses and Elijah, who appeared in glory and spoke of his departure, which he was about to accomplish at Jerusalem. Now Peter and those who were with him were heavy with sleep, but when they became fully awake they saw his glory and the two men who stood with him. And as the men were parting from him, Peter said to Jesus, "Master, it is good that we are here. Let us make three tents, one for you and one for Moses and one for Elijah"— not knowing what he said. As he was saying these things, a cloud came and overshadowed them, and they were afraid as they entered the cloud. And a voice came out of the cloud, saying, "This is my Son, my Chosen One; listen to him!" And when the voice had spoken, Jesus was found alone. And they kept silent and told no one in those days anything of what they had seen. (Luke 9:28–36)

Abba, I went up the mountain to pray, and your glory transfigured my face and my garments. As I partook of the radiance of your glory, I saw with your eyes your love, which shone brightly over the book of my life.

At our meeting, *Abba,* the way of the Passion was illuminated, as I glimpsed the door that opened to heaven. I remained suspended in your presence, in the very heart of the mystery of my unique filiation.

I felt, *Abba,* that I was a mirror of you!

This prompted a more penetrating knowledge of my mission, in the presence of the spokesmen of the law and the prophets. *Abba,* they confirmed my departure, which will take place in Jerusalem.

The three witnesses I chose, *Abba,* although they were exhausted with fatigue, saw that while I was praying the appearance of my face changed, and Moses and Elijah conversed with me.

Peter tried to perpetuate the moment. He did not know what he was saying, *Abba,* for that marvelous moment points to the Resurrection. Your loving fatherhood shapes me, understanding me in the light of your love, into a transfigured existence.

Abba, your goodness is greater than I can conceive!

I heard your voice, *Abba,* coming from the cloud, a sign of your presence. And it surrounded us with its shadow. Peter, John, and James, filled with fear, kept silent. And, once again, you broke your mysterious silence, proclaiming me your Son, your Chosen One, to whom they must listen.

Abba, I bless you for confirming my primary mission, to announce a word that is not mine but yours.

Abba, the mission entrusted to me is brought to life through prayer

When Jesus returned from the mountain accompanied by Peter, James, and John, he found that his followers had not been able to expel a mute and deaf spirit, truly rebellious. The people come to Jesus. When they hear that the young man is suffering unspeakably, they tremble.

They bring the young man to him and begin a dialogue that becomes a catechesis on faith and prayer. The prayer of the father of the young man healed by Jesus has remained as one of the models of Christian prayer. Jesus teaches his own that without prayer it is impossible to overcome the power of evil:

> And when they came to the disciples, they saw a great crowd around them, and scribes arguing with them. And immediately all the crowd, when they saw him, were greatly amazed and ran up to him and greeted him. And he asked them, "What are you arguing about with them?" And someone from the crowd answered him, "Teacher, I

brought my son to you, for he has a spirit that makes him mute. And whenever it seizes him, it throws him down, and he foams and grinds his teeth and becomes rigid. So I asked your disciples to cast it out, and they were not able." And he answered them, "O faithless generation, how long am I to be with you? How long am I to bear with you? Bring him to me." And they brought the boy to him. And when the spirit saw him, immediately it convulsed the boy, and he fell on the ground and rolled about, foaming at the mouth. And Jesus asked his father, "How long has this been happening to him?" And he said, "From childhood. And it has often cast him into fire and into water, to destroy him. But if you can do anything, have compassion on us and help us." And Jesus said to him, "'If you can'! All things are possible for one who believes." Immediately the father of the child cried out and said, "I believe; help my unbelief!" And when Jesus saw that a crowd came running together, he rebuked the unclean spirit, saying to it, "You mute and deaf spirit, I command you, come out of him and never enter him again." And after crying out and convulsing him terribly, it came out, and the boy was like a corpse, so that most of them said, "He is dead." But Jesus took him by the hand and lifted him up, and he arose. And when he had entered the house, his disciples asked him pri-

> vately, "Why could we not cast it out?" And he said to them, "This kind cannot be driven out by anything but prayer." (Mark 9:14–29)

I need to be with you, *Abba*. Prayer is the soul of my life. How I long to bless you! On the way with Peter, James, and John, I saw that they were joyful to follow me. They heard your voice, coming from the cloud, saying that I am your beloved Son.

It was a dazzling moment, *Abba*.

I want to repay you, *Abba*, for the benefits I have received from you. Your goodness is too immense to reciprocate with anything but gratitude. I take my life as a prayer of gratitude.

As I was returning, the people ran to meet me. I met some scholars who were arguing with my disciples, *Abba*. One man told me that he had brought his son possessed by a mute spirit, and had asked that it be cast out, but they were unable to do so. I ordered them to bring him to me and admonished them. I was distressed that, because of their lack of faith, they had not been able to relieve the sick man.

Abba, as soon as the spirit saw me, he violently threw the young man to the ground. My soul sobbed as I saw the suffering of my young brother.

What a disgrace his inability to communicate, to bless and to sing! And you want to reign among men and women, *Abba*, healing them.

His father asked me to take pity on them, hoping

that if I could help them in any way, I would. I questioned him, making him see that everything is possible for those who believe. He shouted that he believed but wanted my help for his lack of faith. I was impressed, *Abba*, by his humility, and he who asks, receives, he who seeks, finds, and to him who knocks, it will be opened.

Abba, I rebuked that unclean spirit to come out of the young man and never again to possess him. He obeyed me, shaking the man so violently that he seemed to have died. I took him by the hand, *Abba,* and, lifting him up, he stood up.

My mother comes to my memory, filled with your grace, *Abba*, with a spontaneity brought about by her awareness of that which is eternal: the sense of truth and goodness. How I love her! Now I contemplate her as I give you thanks for so many blessings received from you, with the confidence that your mercy reaches from generation to generation, to those who are willing to live with reverence in your presence.

This prayer says so much!

She was convinced that you had not asked the impossible of her, *Abba*, you had given it to her, always true to your word. My mother's life has been one of "let it be done."

Later, when I was with my friends, *Abba*, they asked me why they had not been able to expel the spirit as I had. I explained to them that trust in you is the key, and it grows with every encounter with you. I begin and end the day with my eyes turned toward you. I need to be with you to receive your peace, to see things from your light.

Prayer is the door, *Abba*, but it is not improvised, it is prepared, it leads to the surrender of what has been undertaken. That is why I answered them that this kind cannot be delivered with anything but prayer.

Abba, the mission entrusted to me is brought to life through prayer.

Abba, I shared your wonderful joy

Jesus was happy that publicans and sinners sought him out to listen to him. On the other hand, some Pharisees and scribes murmured since his conduct scandalized them, for he welcomed and ate with sinners, whom they despised as impure scum who did not observe the law in its integrity.

Jesus felt harassed by those self-righteous people who considered themselves to be just. And, with marvelous inspiration and determined to shake them and make them reflect on their attitude, he told them a parable, one that revealed the heart of God. With this parable — the most beautiful parable ever imagined! — he respectfully defended himself.

It was a unique experience that opened the way to a new understanding of the Father, which attracted and fascinated the outcasts. It sprouted from that relationship with God whom he called, *Abba*. Such an image reveals a perfect knowledge of the love of his *Abba*, of the mystery which condenses everything: God is love.

Jesus describes the foundation of the dignity of every human being: divine filiation. He always looks to the cause of causes: the love of his *Abba*, who created us out of love and to love.

> And he said, "There was a man who had two sons. And the younger of them said to his father, 'Father, give me the share of property that is coming to me.' And he divided his property between them. Not many days later, the younger son gathered all he had and took a journey into a far country, and there he squandered his property in reckless living. And when he had spent everything, a severe famine arose in that country, and he began to be in need. So he went and hired himself out to one of the citizens of that country, who sent him into his fields to feed pigs. And he was longing to be fed with the pods that the pigs ate, and no one gave him anything.
>
> "But when he came to himself, he said, 'How many of my father's hired servants have more than enough bread, but I perish here with hunger! I will arise and go to my father, and I will say to him, "Father, I have sinned against heaven and before you. I am no longer worthy to be called your son. Treat me as one of your hired servants."' And he arose and came to his father. But while he was still a long way off, his father saw him and felt compassion, and ran and embraced him and kissed him. And the son said to

him, 'Father, I have sinned against heaven and before you. I am no longer worthy to be called your son.' But the father said to his servants, 'Bring quickly the best robe, and put it on him, and put a ring on his hand, and shoes on his feet. And bring the fattened calf and kill it, and let us eat and celebrate. For this my son was dead, and is alive again; he was lost, and is found.' And they began to celebrate.

"Now his older son was in the field, and as he came and drew near to the house, he heard music and dancing. And he called one of the servants and asked what these things meant. And he said to him, 'Your brother has come, and your father has killed the fattened calf, because he has received him back safe and sound.' But he was angry and refused to go in. His father came out and entreated him, but he answered his father, 'Look, these many years I have served you, and I never disobeyed your command, yet you never gave me a young goat, that I might celebrate with my friends. But when this son of yours came, who has devoured your property with prostitutes, you killed the fattened calf for him!' And he said to him, 'Son, you are always with me, and all that is mine is yours. It was fitting to celebrate and be glad, for this your brother was dead, and is alive; he was lost, and is found.'" (Luke 15:11–32)

Abba, thank you. In the silence of your intimacy, in

prayer, I am amazed to have preached something like this, for I have painted a perfect portrait of you. I felt I was not only your beloved Son, but also your Word.

Abba, because you are love, you can only act by loving!

When I was an adolescent visiting Jerusalem on the occasion of the Passover, faced with my mother's reprimands, I explained to her my encounter with you in the midst of the teachers. I woke up from being a child, *Abba*, and, realizing that I was a young man with infinite tasks, I asked her two questions. When I referred to you as my Father, I looked at Joseph and smiled at him. He bowed his head with tears in his eyes.

This childhood memory left a mark on me, for could I call you that without his example, *Abba*? Always sensitive to your blessings, he always told me to thank you because you are good, because your love is eternal. He and my mother taught me to make my life a prayer of gratitude.

Abba, your paternal heart sustains my trust in you. I bless you from the depths of my soul. You are a Father who listens and watches, you are always with me.

Abba, I love who I am and what I am!

The experience of being loved by you means that I find myself to be lovable. I feel free as the wind, *Abba*, as I take on the goodness of my mission: to be light, to give encouragement, to make people see what is truly valuable in life.

In your presence, I tell you that I am committed to

my neediest brothers and sisters, *Abba*. They ignore the complicated precepts of the legists. It is impossible for them to comply with them. Something alive in my spirit prompts me to summon them around me as I perceive them weary and tired.

You were waiting for the return of your youngest son. You never lost faith in him. Nor in the older one, who even accused you of being miserly, whom you begged to share in the joy of the encounter. You teach us, *Abba*, that to love means to give yourself to the one you love in order to inspire love in his heart.

And how many times I have asked you how to convey your joy! I was able to understand it when I showed them your heart, for I saw how you rejoiced when you found your son who was lost. Thank you, *Abba*, for allowing me to understand and share your wonderful joy.

Why, *Abba*, why?

Jesus was walking near Solomon's Portico, on the feast of the Dedication. He felt confronted in the midst of a storm that preluded his passion, surrounded by a group of Jewish brothers who demanded him to tell them if he was the Messiah. He replied to those who subjected him to such interrogation, reminding them that he had already told them, but they did not believe in the works he performed. Jesus declared that he and his Father were one. His accusers wanted to apprehend him:

> At that time the Feast of Dedication took place at Jerusalem. It was winter, and Jesus was walking in the temple, in the colonnade of Solomon. So the Jews gathered around him and said to him, "How long will you keep us in suspense? If you are the Christ, tell us plainly." Jesus answered them, "I told you, and you do not believe. The works that I do in my Father's name bear witness about me, but you do not believe because

you are not among my sheep. My sheep hear my voice, and I know them, and they follow me. I give them eternal life, and they will never perish, and no one will snatch them out of my hand. My Father, who has given them to me, is greater than all, and no one is able to snatch them out of the Father's hand. I and the Father are one."

The Jews picked up stones again to stone him. Jesus answered them, "I have shown you many good works from the Father; for which of them are you going to stone me?" The Jews answered him, "It is not for a good work that we are going to stone you but for blasphemy, because you, being a man, make yourself God." Jesus answered them, "Is it not written in your Law, 'I said, you are gods'? If he called them gods to whom the word of God came — and Scripture cannot be broken — do you say of him whom the Father consecrated and sent into the world, 'You are blaspheming', because I said, 'I am the Son of God'? If I am not doing the works of my Father, then do not believe me; but if I do them, even though you do not believe me, believe the works, that you may know and understand that the Father is in me and I am in the Father." Again they sought to arrest him, but he escaped from their hands. (John 10:22–39)

Abba, they confronted me, demanding to know if I was

the One sent by you. I exhorted them to observe the works that I carry out in your name, for they are the ones that bear witness to me, to your saving presence.

It was impossible to convince them! I cannot force them, *Abba*, because love does not impose obligations, nor does it use force to demand a response.

Abba, as I grasped the reality that you and I are one, I felt so close to you.

They considered it a scandal. They wanted to stone me, *Abba*. And strengthened by a miraculous serenity, I confronted them, affirming that I had shown them many good works, until I ended up asking which one of these works they wanted to stone me for.

At last, I escaped from their hands. I am overwhelmed. Why, *Abba*, why?

Abba, take this cup from me, but not what I will, but what you will

---

In Gethsemane a terrifying event takes place. Jesus, the prophet of Nazareth, anointed by God with the Holy Spirit and power, the evangelist who proclaims the coming of the Kingdom, the teacher full of wisdom and authority, the friend of the outcasts, publicans and sinners, the exorcist, the thaumaturge who has dominion over nature, disease, and even death, has fallen to the ground and fallen again, seized by fear.

Yet, at one point, he shows his trust in the love and power of the Father, whom he invokes as *Abba*. His prayer becomes a supplication, and ends in unreserved abandonment, in unconditional acceptance:

> And they went to a place called Gethsemane. And he said to his disciples, "Sit here while I pray." And he took with him Peter and James and John, and began to be greatly distressed and troubled. And he said to them, "My soul is very sorrowful, even to death. Remain here and

watch." And going a little farther, he fell on the ground and prayed that, if it were possible, the hour might pass from him. And he said, "Abba, Father, all things are possible for you. Remove this cup from me. Yet not what I will, but what you will." And he came and found them sleeping, and he said to Peter, "Simon, are you asleep? Could you not watch one hour? Watch and pray that you may not enter into temptation. The spirit indeed is willing, but the flesh is weak." And again he went away and prayed, saying the same words. And again he came and found them sleeping, for their eyes were very heavy, and they did not know what to answer him. And he came the third time and said to them, "Are you still sleeping and taking your rest? It is enough; the hour has come. The Son of Man is betrayed into the hands of sinners. Rise, let us be going; see, my betrayer is at hand." (Mark 14:32–42)

Abba, I am troubled, overcome by the deepest sorrow. Mortal terror is descending upon me.

I feel so fragile, *Abba.*

I asked Peter, James, and John to sit and watch with me while I prayed, *Abba.* They are the witnesses of my power over death and, above all, of the predilection you have for me.

I have never before been so pierced by my humanity. I leap and I go forward, and I fall and fall again, with my insides broken, in the most vivid experience of my passion. I beg you to take this cup away from me, but not what I want, but what you want, *Abba*.

Prayer is an essential part of my ministry, *Abba*.

I go in search of them and find them asleep. I turn to Simon. I ask him to watch and pray, for the spirit is ready and the flesh is weak. I turn away, and with greater insistence I tell you again to take this cup away from me, but not what I want, but what you want, *Abba*.

Once again, I go in search of them, and find them asleep, not knowing what to say to me. And, for the third time, enough is enough, I tell them that they can sleep and rest. Now I abandon myself into your hands, *Abba*.

The hour has come, *Abba*, to be delivered into the hands of sinners. I feel abandoned and yet, *Abba*, I continue to trust in you!

My thoughts follow silent paths, which surprisingly lead to an ocean of peace. My soul and my path are illuminated, sustained by your love. This is a mystery, *Abba*, but, if of anything I have no doubt, it is that life has the last word, my resurrection will be the triumph over all these limitations.

Abba, I now understand with my life what I have revealed

The plot to arrest Jesus began to be carried out. This was plotted by the high priests and the elders in union with Judas Iscariot, one of the Twelve.

Jesus assumes his fate to die, which corresponds to God's design as manifested in the Scriptures. It is he, and not those who come with swords and sticks, who controls the situation.

Jesus' last words to the cruel traitor are like a true song of his compassion:

> While he was still speaking, Judas came, one of the twelve, and with him a great crowd with swords and clubs, from the chief priests and the elders of the people. Now the betrayer had given them a sign, saying, "The one I will kiss is the man; seize him." And he came up to Jesus at once and said, "Greetings, Rabbi!" And he kissed him. Jesus said to him, "Friend, do what you came to do." Then they came up and laid hands on Jesus

> and seized him. And behold, one of those who were with Jesus stretched out his hand and drew his sword and struck the servant of the high priest and cut off his ear. Then Jesus said to him, "Put your sword back into its place. For all who take the sword will perish by the sword. Do you think that I cannot appeal to my Father, and he will at once send me more than twelve legions of angels? But how then should the Scriptures be fulfilled, that it must be so?" At that hour Jesus said to the crowds, "Have you come out as against a robber, with swords and clubs to capture me? Day after day I sat in the temple teaching, and you did not seize me. But all this has taken place that the Scriptures of the prophets might be fulfilled." Then all the disciples left him and fled. (Matthew 26:47–56)

Abba, as I am led to the palace of the high priest, abandoned by all, I acknowledge before you how much I loved Judas Iscariot in silence!

He was driven by a wild enthusiasm, *Abba*, frequented by the complicity of evil and in opposition to the dynamism of your kingdom. He was threatened by the light of truth, consumed by the idea which could never convince him of what he considered to be an upside-down messianism.

It terrifies me, *Abba*, just to imagine the distant exile of the darkness outside, infested by weeping and grinding of teeth.

When I was still a child, I remember being restless, staring at the flames of the fireplace in my home, thinking of that endless wandering, which gave rise to a tremendous horror in me. My mother's eyes and mine met. *Abba*, under the glow of her eyes, I found comfort. She, without uttering a word, told me that, for you, nothing is impossible.

Abba, I have never denied the existence of Hades, the place of eternal punishment, but will there be anyone in it?

At last Judas came out of hiding, *Abba*, and sold me for the price of a slave. Now, he flees; I feel the rumor of an inconsolable emptiness. I perceive the depths of evil, and suddenly I see myself in the heart of an infinite present. He tells me about his life. He sees he is persecuted by himself, dull and restless. The anointing of the Spirit leads me to liberate Judas Iscariot.

And I hear him say for the first time since I called him to follow me: "Thank you Lord." And between amazement and enthusiasm, *Abba*, our eyes meet in the loving bond of divine living. Is not forgiveness the most beautiful name of love?

Abba, I now understand with my life what I have revealed to the world.

Abba, I promised the repentant criminal that today he would be with me in paradise

Jesus, who went about doing good, and from whose eyes flowed rivers of compassion as he healed all those oppressed by the devil, is on the cross mistreated, suffering unspeakable torture, with his beard covered with spittle.

The authorities challenged him saying that, if he was the Messiah of God and had saved others, he should save himself. The soldiers rebuked him and asked why he didn't save himself, if he was the king of the Jews. One of the criminals insulted him and told him that, if he was the Messiah, he should save himself as well as them.

The other man who was crucified took pity on Jesus and defended him, asking the criminal if he did not even fear God, suffering the same torture. Severity and compassion came together. Compassion appeared in an unexpected corner: the heart of the good thief.

And, this sinner, humbly accepting his guilt, calling Jesus by name, begged him to remember him when he would come in to his kingdom.

Jesus, even on the cross, showed unfailing mercy, responding out of forgiveness by opening the gates of paradise to the repentant sinner.

Jesus reigns from a cross:

> And when they came to the place that is called The Skull, there they crucified him, and the criminals, one on his right and one on his left. And Jesus said, "Father, forgive them, for they know not what they do." And they cast lots to divide his garments. And the people stood by, watching, but the rulers scoffed at him, saying, "He saved others; let him save himself, if he is the Christ of God, his Chosen One!" The soldiers also mocked him, coming up and offering him sour wine and saying, "If you are the King of the Jews, save yourself!" There was also an inscription over him, "This is the King of the Jews." One of the criminals who were hanged railed at him, saying, "Are you not the Christ? Save yourself and us!" But the other rebuked him, saying, "Do you not fear God, since you are under the same sentence of condemnation? And we indeed justly, for we are receiving the due reward of our deeds; but this man has done nothing wrong." And he said, "Jesus, remember me when you come into your kingdom." And he said to him, "Truly, I say to you, today you will be with me in

paradise." (Luke 23:33–43)

Abba, an anguishing pain makes me feel abandoned. But a sense of peace strokes my soul, knowing that I am in your hands and that you hear me when I call upon you.

From my misery, crushed and naked, I implore, *Abba*, your forgiveness for those who destroy my body, reflecting the darkness of their heart. The freedom with which you have created them is complex. And their rescue is exercised in forgiveness.

Yes, *Abba*, forgiveness appeases, heals, restores, and redeems!

I have grown up with a memory that marked me, *Abba*. I see my parents talking when I returned from the holy city as a young boy. Joseph, with his ability to see clearly and express himself without words, helped my mother understand that my behavior had surprised him. Mum, in a flash of clairvoyance, replied that if I was a mystery to him, I was even more of a mystery to her, and even more so to myself, to the point of assuring him that I carried with me a mystery impossible to share.

This mystery gives me a clear sense of identity, *Abba*. At last, I understand it, as I promise this good repentant sinner that today he will be with me in paradise.

Thank you, *Abba*, for listening to me

A muffled moan emanated from his fragile, exhausted, and beaten body. And in spite of everything, the goodness that identified him did not die, throbbing in the depths of his being, as he performed the supreme act of charity: to give his life. His heart, certainly, stopped, but he never stopped loving:

> After this, Jesus, knowing that all was now finished, said (to fulfill the Scripture), "I thirst." A jar full of sour wine stood there, so they put a sponge full of the sour wine on a hyssop branch and held it to his mouth. When Jesus had received the sour wine, he said, "It is finished," and he bowed his head and gave up his spirit. (John 19:28–30)

Abba, I have carried out your will in every moment of my life. I have grown in the light of your grace and reached perfection. Now that everything has been accomplished, I know that you have heard my prayer. A sense of peace overcomes me in the midst of the most excruciating pain. All that remains for me to say to you, *Abba*, from the beginning and perfection of faith, in the overall perspective, an eternal feeling reveals to me that no one is taking my life from me, so I bow my head and give you my spirit.

Thank you, *Abba,* for listening to me!

In preparation for the Jubilee Year 2025, the Exploring Prayer series delves into the various dimensions of prayer in the Christian life. These brief, accessible books can help you learn to dialogue with God and rediscover the beauty of trusting in the Lord with humility and joy.

Prayer Today: A Challenge to Overcome
Notes on Prayer: Volume 1
by Angelo Comastri
In order to have saints, what is needed are people of authentic prayer, and authentic prayer is that which inflames with a fire of love. Only in this way is it possible to lift the world and bring it near to the heart of God. To pray in truth, we must present ourselves before God with the open wounds of our smallness and our sin. Only in this way will the encounter with God be an encounter of liberation and redemption.

Praying with the Psalms
Notes on Prayer: Volume 2
by Gianfranco Ravasi
This little guide to the Psalms includes four cardinal points: a general reflection on prayer, the breath of the soul; a panoramic look at the psalmic texts; a portrait of the two protagonists, God and the worshipper, but also the intrusion of the presence of evil; and finally, an anthology of brief commentaries on the Psalms most dear to tradition and the liturgy. The hope is that all the faithful may draw fully from this wonderful treasury of prayers.

The Jesus Prayer
Notes on Prayer: Volume 3
by Juan Lopez Vergara
This book explores the unique experience of the fatherhood of God for Jesus Christ, whom he calls Abba — which in his native Aramaic language means "Dad." Throughout his earthly life, Jesus is in contact dialogue with Abba. From his Baptism in the Jordan through his public ministry and ultimately his crucifixion, this relationship will mark him forever, transforming his life, and our lives, too.

Praying with Saints and Sinners
Notes on Prayer: Volume 4
by Paul Brendan Murray
The saints whose writings on prayer and meditation

are explored in this book are among the most celebrated in the great spiritual tradition. The aim of this book is to discover what help the great saints can offer those of us who desire to make progress in the life of prayer, but who find ourselves being constantly deflected from our purpose, our tentative efforts undermined perhaps most of all by human weakness.

Parables on Prayer
Notes on Prayer: Volume 5
by Anthony Pitta
What characterizes, in a singular way, Jesus's teaching on prayer is the recourse to parables. Jesus did not invent a new system for praying. Jesus was not a hermit, a Buddhist monk, or a yogi. He instead chose the daily life of his people to teach prayer with parables. This book explores the parables in the Gospels explicitly related to prayer. The reader is guided by Jesus, the original teacher of prayer with parables.

The Church in Prayer
Notes on Prayer: Volume 6
by Carthusian Monks
Carthusian Monks reside in several international monasteries. Founded in 1084 by Saint Bruno, the Order of Carthusians are dedicated to prayer, in silence, in community. Like other cloistered religious, the Carthusians live a life focused on prayer and contemplation.

The Prayer of Mary and the Saints
Notes on Prayer: Volume 7
by Catherine Aubin
When Mary appears, anywhere in the whole world, the places where she appears have points in common with the biblical places where she stayed and lived. This book reviews these places, examining what they reveal to us about Mary's identity, and what the inner spaces are that Mary asks us to dwell in today. This book also explores the unique relationship two holy women each had with Mary, leading us toward a new, deep revelation of Mary's closeness to each of us.

The Prayer Jesus Taught Us: The "Our Father"
Notes on Prayer: Volume 8
by Hugh Vanni
This book identifies the theological-biblical structure underlying the Lord's Prayer and situates it in the living environment of the early Church. This will give us a framework of reference, and as a result we will see first the antecedents in Mark, then the systematic presentation of Matthew, Paul's push forward, the accentuation of Luke, and, finally, the mature synthesis found in John.